Inside Your Insides
A Guide to the Microbes
That Call You Home

Written by **Claire Eamer**

Illustrated by **Marie-Ève Tremblay**

Kids Can Press

To my son, Patrick, who introduced me to more microbes than I'd believed possible — C.E.

To Lou and Bob, for giving me a strong immune system — M.T.

Acknowledgments
My thanks to research assistant Alan Daley, and to Laura Wegener Parfrey of the University of British Columbia for casting an expert eye over the manuscript.

Kids Can Press acknowledges the financial support of the Government of Ontario, through the Ontario Media Development Corporation's Ontario Book Initiative; the Ontario Arts Council; the Canada Council for the Arts; and the Government of Canada, through the CBF, for our publishing activity.

Published in Canada by	Published in the U.S. by
Kids Can Press Ltd.	Kids Can Press Ltd.
25 Dockside Drive	2250 Military Road
Toronto, ON M5A 0B5	Tonawanda, NY 14150

www.kidscanpress.com

Edited by Valerie Wyatt and Stacey Roderick
Designed by Julia Naimska

This book is smyth sewn casebound.
Manufactured in Shenzhen, China, in 3/2016 by C & C Offset

CM 16 0 9 8 7 6 5 4 3 2 1

Library and Archives Canada Cataloguing in Publication

Eamer, Claire, 1947–, author
        Inside your insides : a guide to the microbes that call you home / written by Claire Eamer ; illustrated by Marie-Ève Tremblay.

Includes index.
ISBN 978-1-77138-332-5 (bound)

1. Microorganisms — Juvenile literature. 2. Bacteria — Juvenile literature. 3. Microbiology — Juvenile literature. I. Tremblay, Marie-Ève, 1978 July 19–, illustrator II. Title.

QR57.E26 2016   j579   C2015-907019-8

Kids Can Press is a *Corus*™ Entertainment company

Table of Contents

Meet Your Microbiome!

You might think you're alone, but you're not. Ever. Wherever you go, tiny hitchhikers tag along for the ride. Some have been hanging around your body since before you were born, and some are climbing aboard right now — maybe even from the pages of this book.

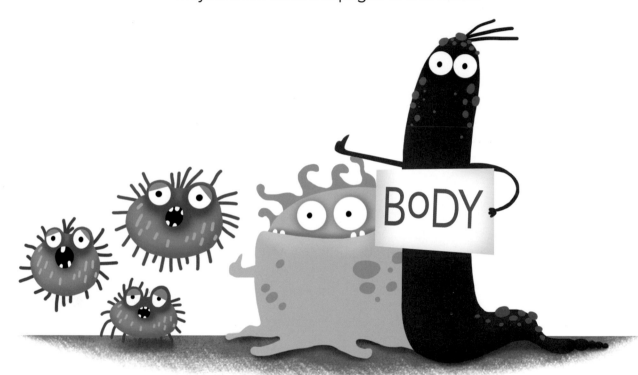

But don't panic. Most of them are harmless.

The hitchhikers are actually microbes — tiny living things so small that you need a microscope to see them. And every person carries around trillions and trillions of these critters. They are part of what scientists call your microbiome (MY-croh-BY-ome).

A biome is a group of plants, animals and other organisms (living things) that all live in a similar kind of place. The tropical rainforest and the arctic tundra are examples of different biomes. A microbiome is much the same, except the organisms are microscopic, and the place is a lot smaller, too. It might even be a living creature, such as a dog, a mouse — or you.

Where will you find your collection of microbes? Everywhere!

They're inside and outside of you, in your nose and mouth, in your lungs, between your toes, in your hair and eyelashes, and snuggled in the warm hollow behind your ears. And a huge number of microbes live in your gut. Just as in the rainforest, where some kinds of organisms live in the treetops and others down in the tree roots, different kinds of microbes settle in the places that suit them best.

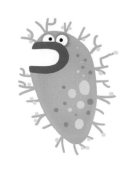

Did You Know?

It's not really possible to count the microbes — or the cells — in a human body. You can only take an educated guess. Currently, the best guesses place the number of microbes in the average adult human between 100 trillion and 200 trillion. That's a lot! If you counted all day and all night, every day, it would take you more than 3000 years just to get to 100 trillion.

In some ways, you might even be more microbe than you are human. Scientists estimate that for every human cell in your body, there's at least one microbe cell and maybe as many as ten. But those microbes aren't alien invaders. The truth is you need them, and they need you. Microbes and humans have been together for so long that we depend on each other to survive. So, in a way, microbes are us!

What Are Microbes?

Most of the microscopic organisms traveling in you and on you are just a single cell, or something even smaller. Some can make you sick, and others do little more than hang out and keep you company. But plenty of microbes are actually good for you. They help you digest food, train your immune system to fight disease, produce chemicals that keep you healthy, or even form protective layers that block other, more harmful microbes.

All microbes are small, but that doesn't mean they're all the same. Here's a guide to the most common microbial hitchhikers.

Bacteria (bak-TEE-ree-ah): These single-celled organisms are found almost everywhere on Earth, from deep underground to high in the sky. A few are big enough to be seen with the naked eye, but the bacteria in your microbiome are much smaller than that. In fact, several hundred thousand of them would fit on the pointy end of a pin. There are more bacteria on Earth than any other kind of organism, and they are probably the most common kind of microbe in your microbiome!

Bacteria

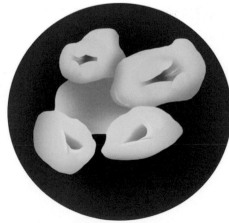

Archaea

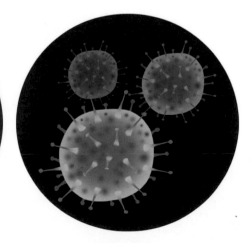

Viruses

Archaea (ar-KEE-ah): This is another group of single-celled organisms, but they are not closely related to bacteria. Archaea are experts at surviving in tough places — one kind can even live in acid strong enough to eat through metal. Others, though, hang out in comfier places, such as your belly button.

Viruses (VY-russ-ez): Smaller than a cell, each one is just a few scraps of genetic code inside a protective coating. The virus that causes the common cold contains only 10 genes, compared to the 20 000 genes in a human cell. Viruses can't make energy or reproduce on their own. Instead, they invade a cell and trick it into making copies of the virus. Sometimes the copies slip out through the cell wall and go in search of more cells to invade. Sometimes the cell just keeps creating viruses until it explodes, spreading viruses everywhere.

Fungi (FUN-jee): This group includes everything from single yeast cells to huge mushrooms. The fungi in and on your body are the single-celled variety that adore warm, damp spots like the spaces between your toes.

Protists (PROH-tists): These tiny, single-celled relatives of fungi, animals and plants are bigger than a lot of other microbes but still microscopic. Some protists cause serious diseases, but many of them just live with us as part of us.

Mites: Relatives of spiders and scorpions, mites are the giants of your microbiome, but you still need a microscope to see them. They're especially fond of hair follicles and the oil glands in your skin.

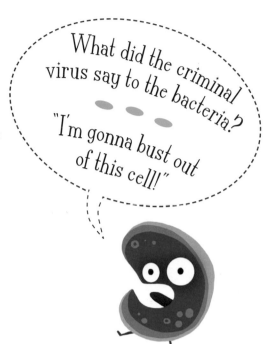

What did the criminal virus say to the bacteria?

"I'm gonna bust out of this cell!"

Fungi

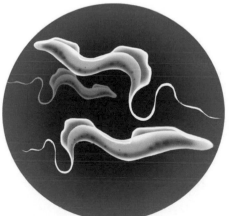

Protists

Mites

We Are Not Alone

Not sure you like your microbes?

— — —

Don't worry — they'll grow on you!

Right about now, you might be thinking, "Yuck! Why are all these bugs picking on me?" Well, don't worry. You're not alone. Everyone and everything on Earth is in the same boat. We live in an invisible sea of microbes. They're in the air, the water, the soil and every living thing.

And they've been here for a long, long time.

In fact, the first living things on Earth were microbes. Organisms that contain lots of cells — from dandelions to dinosaurs to people — didn't come along until a couple of billion years later.

We owe a great deal to those tiny, ancient cells — especially a group called cyanobacteria (sy-AN-oh-bak-TEE-ree-ah). They were the first Earth organisms to use the Sun's energy to run their own little cellular engines, just as plants do today. When they appeared in Earth's oceans — at least 2.5 billion years ago — there was little or no life on land and nothing of any size in the oceans. But cyanobacteria transformed the planet.

They floated through the sea, gobbling up sunlight and minerals and pumping out waste products. One of the waste products was oxygen. For hundreds of millions of years, waste oxygen slowly seeped into Earth's oceans and atmosphere. And just as slowly, new creatures evolved — creatures that needed oxygen to live. That includes most of the animals alive today, both on land and in water. And it includes us. Without the oxygen produced by ocean microbes, we wouldn't exist.

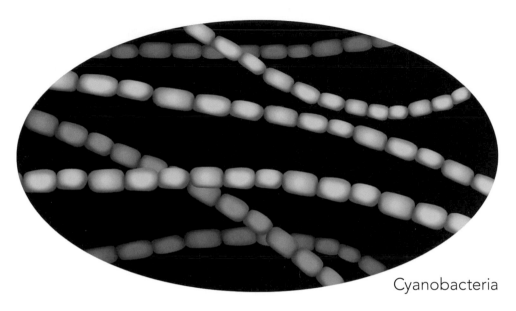
Cyanobacteria

Fortunately, bacteria are still pumping oxygen into our atmosphere. Ocean microbes produce half the world's oxygen. The other half comes from plants on land, which contain oxygen-producing microbes of their own. Without microbes, we wouldn't have anything to breathe.

We also wouldn't have anything to eat. Plants can't grow without the help of microbes in the soil, and bacteria in their tissues help to capture the Sun's energy. Animals depend on microbes, too. The tiny animals that eat microbes are in turn eaten by bigger animals, all the way through the food web to the animals we eat (and a few animals that might like to eat us). If all the world's microbes disappeared tomorrow, other living things would disappear soon afterward. Including people.

So respect your microbes. You owe them a lot!

Did You Know?

Some bacteria can eat electricity. They gobble up electrons given off by rocks and minerals, especially in the muck at the bottom of the sea. Micro-zap!

The War Against Microbes

Did You Know?

More than 330 years ago, there lived a Dutchman, Antoni van Leeuwenhoek, who was fascinated by the world he saw through his handmade microscopes. One day, he squinted at a drop of water through one of his lenses and saw tiny creatures, wriggling and spinning and busily living their lives. It was the first time anyone had seen microbes. He began searching for microbes everywhere, even in guck scraped from people's teeth. And what a treasure he found in the mouths of two old men who had never used a toothbrush! Their guck seethed with tiny, squirming creatures. Van Leeuwenhoek had just discovered bacteria — living in people!

We are walking microbiomes, part microbe and part human. But we haven't always been kind to our microbe side. Although to be fair, for a long time we didn't know our microbes even existed. They were just too small for us to see.

Once we had microscopes, though, we discovered a whole world of microbes. Still, nobody thought they were important, because how could something that small possibly affect a person?

Then everything changed about 150 years ago. That's when scientists discovered that some microbes — they called them germs — could cause serious diseases in humans. And that's when we declared war on microbes.

It made sense: if you got rid of germs, you would get rid of disease. It was a great idea that led to important changes, such as cleaner homes and hospitals, better sewage and garbage systems, and the development of new medicines — especially penicillin and other antibiotics — that attacked disease-causing bacteria.

But we went too far. It turned out that our microbiomes are far more complicated than we realized. A lot of those microbes keep us healthy. We need them, and yet we were killing them off along with the bad microbes.

Today, scientists are trying to understand how our microbiomes work and how to help them work well. That means going back to the beginning, to where our microbes come from.

Did You Know?

What's the difference between a microbe and a germ? Not much. Both are names for tiny, mostly single-celled organisms. Some make us sick, but most don't. But because we usually think of a germ as something that makes us sick, we're using the word *microbe* in this book.

The Making of Our Microbiome

We collect microbes from everything we touch, eat or get close to. And that process starts even before we're born.

People used to think that babies were free of microbes until they made their journey down their mother's birth canal, where they picked up some of her microbes. But recently, some Spanish researchers found microbes in meconium, a newborn baby's first poop. Not long after that, some American scientists found microbes in placentas, the organs that nourish babies inside their mothers' bodies. From these two discoveries, the scientists realized that babies collect microbes even in the months before they are born.

What's the first lesson in microbe business school?

How to cell yourself!

But where do those microbes come from? Scientists found that the mix of microbes in newborn babies is similar to the mix found in an adult's mouth, rather than in the birth canal. Somehow, microbes from the mother's mouth travel through her body and affect the microbiome of her unborn baby.

After birth, babies pick up more microbes quickly. By the time a baby is one month old, a tiny bit of its poop — just enough to cover the tip of a small spoon — already contains a trillion microbes.

As you grow older, you collect more and more microbes, from many different sources. Every time you take a breath, you inhale thousands of spores, the little reproductive forms of fungi. Every bite you eat contains bacteria, archaea and viruses. When you pet a puppy, go to school, play at the beach or visit a friend's house, you collect even more microbes.

Your body's collection of mites grows more slowly. You pick them up from contact with other people. Babies love nuzzling — rubbing their faces against their parents. In the process, the baby picks up tiny mites that settle into hair follicles and oil glands. When the baby grows into a teenager or young adult and snuggles with a girlfriend or boyfriend, he or she picks up another dose of mites. By the time we're adults, we all have our own population of mites.

Some of Your Microbes Are Bad Guys

Not every microbe in your microbiome is your friend. One-quarter of all infectious diseases are caused by microbes. That includes some really serious diseases, such as tuberculosis, as well as others — the common cold, for example — that are just messy and annoying.

Remember the two old men who never brushed their teeth? Some of the tiny, wriggly bacteria in their mouths were troublemakers that cause toothaches, cavities and gum disease. By the time those men met Antoni van Leeuwenhoek and his microscope, they probably didn't have a full set of teeth between them.

Knock, knock!
Who's there?

• • •

Germ.
Germ who?
Germ-mind if I come in?

Bacteria can cause anything from bad breath to a deadly plague. In the 1300s, a sickness called the Black Death swept across Asia and Europe. It killed millions of people on both continents, including as many as a third of the people living in Europe at the time. The villain was a bacterium called *Yersinia pestis* or *Y. pestis*.

The *Y. pestis* bacteria got into rats, mice and other small animals and made them sick. Fleas spread the disease by sucking up infected blood from one animal and passing some of the bacteria along to the next animal they bit. Sometimes that next victim was human. In people, *Y. pestis* causes plague, and once people catch it, the plague can spread quickly. Sick people coughed out droplets containing the bacteria, other people breathed them in, and they, too, got sick. And so the disease continued to spread, killing as it went.

Viruses sometimes spread through coughing, too. Human rhinovirus, the virus that causes most head colds, spreads by making your nose run. Then you cough and sneeze and drip, spreading virus-laden mucus about. People breathe in droplets of the mucus or touch them — and the virus has a new victim.

Fungi can also be bad guys — or, at least, very annoying guys. A common kind of fungus produces dandruff, which makes your scalp itch and flake. Another kind of fungus causes athlete's foot, which can produce cracks in the skin between your toes.

Some protists can do serious damage. Malaria, which makes millions of people sick each year and kills hundreds of thousands, is caused by a tiny protist passed to people through a mosquito bite.

Did You Know?

The memory of the Black Death is still with us. The nursery rhyme "Ring Around the Rosie" began as a verse describing symptoms of the plague. And we still tell the legend of the Pied Piper of Hamelin, who piped the rats out of town to save the townsfolk from the Black Death.

And Some of Your Microbes Are Good Guys

Did You Know?

According to a 2015 report, the world champions of microbiome variety are the Yanomami people, who live in the Amazon jungle. Their microbiomes contain many different kinds of microbes — far more than any human biome that's been studied before.

A lot of the microbes in your body are actually good guys. In fact, some of them fight off the bad-guy microbes or at least keep them under control. Bacteriophages — phages (FAY-jez) for short — are an example. They're viruses that infect and kill bacteria, including some kinds of bacteria that make us sick.

Phages were discovered during World War I by a Canadian doctor named Félix d'Hérelle. He was trying to find a way to treat dysentery, a dangerous kind of diarrhea that was making soldiers sick and even killing them. D'Hérelle was growing dysentery bacteria in his lab, but something was killing them — something too small to see. He realized that a virus was attacking the bacteria, and he found a way to turn it into a medicine for the sick soldiers. It saved a lot of lives.

After the war, d'Hérelle developed more medicines using phages. However, researchers still didn't really understand viruses, and doctors were uneasy about giving patients medicine they didn't understand. Then penicillin and other antibiotics came along. They were cheaper and easier to make, and they worked. Today, however, when antibiotics aren't always effective, scientists are taking another look at phages.

Even though bacteria get a bad name for causing disease, most bacteria actually do good things for us. Some are even your first line of defence. Bacteria on your skin gobble up the waxy stuff that skin cells produce and make an oily substance that helps keep your skin from drying and cracking. That's important because cracks in your skin are wide-open doors to some of the nasty bacteria that can make you sick.

But the real treasure trove of bacteria is in your gut — your digestive system. It's teeming with bacteria that work away at the food you eat, gobbling up things your digestive system can't handle and producing waste products that your body actually can absorb. According to one estimate, as much as 10 percent of your body's energy is produced by gut microbes. Microbes also break down the waste materials in your gut, using some of them as food and turning the rest into a form your body can get rid of easily — poop! In fact, a lot of microbes leave your body every day, as part of your poop.

Did You Know?

Even bad guys can be good guys sometimes. Human rhinovirus can give you a terrible cold, but not always. About 4 out of 10 people who have the virus in their systems don't get sick. Instead, their immune systems block the virus. Exposure to not-too-serious germs such as rhinovirus can help keep your immune system ready to fight off much more dangerous microbes.

Your Body Is a World

Just for a moment, think about your body from a microbe's point of view. Ready?

Big, isn't it? Big enough to be a home to billions and trillions of microbe-sized organisms.

And there are plenty of different landscapes to choose from. Wide, open plains along the forearms and legs. Deep valleys behind the ears and in the belly button. Sheltering forests in the hair. Cozy caves in the pores and hair follicles. Lovely, warm, swampy areas between the legs. And a huge, dark, warm, food-filled world beneath the surface — the gut, with everything a microbe could want in life. At least, everything a lot of microbes want.

Each of us is a whole, huge world to our microbes. Just like Earth, we have different landscapes that attract different kinds of critters. And even landscapes that look similar can have plenty of variety.

For example, if you saw a picture of an empty plain, you might not know where it was. But add a herd of grazing bison, and you'd know it was in North America. A bouncing mob of kangaroos would mean Australia. A pride of lions would mean Africa. The landscape might look similar, but the mix of organisms varies depending on location, climate, history and the long process of evolution.

Exactly what microbes settle in the body's landscapes depends on just as many factors. Take tongue microbes, for example. The mix of microbes on your tongue is probably pretty similar to the mix on your best friend's tongue. But that mix won't be exactly the same. The differences will depend on what you inherited or picked up from your family, what foods you eat, what microbes are floating around the places you live in and visit, your own genetic makeup and immune system, and plenty of other factors.

But one thing is for sure. Your tongue microbes and your friend's tongue microbes will be very different from your eyebrow microbes. (Yup, there are microbes there, too!)

Basically, the human microbiome is complicated — and the more we learn, the more complicated it seems.

Did You Know?

Microbiome cheese, anyone? Recently, a microbiologist and an artist collected bacteria from the mouths and toes of several people, grew batches of bacteria and used them — along with milk — to make cheese. The cheese was displayed at a science museum in Ireland. Some of it was even served up to visitors, including the people who contributed their bacteria.

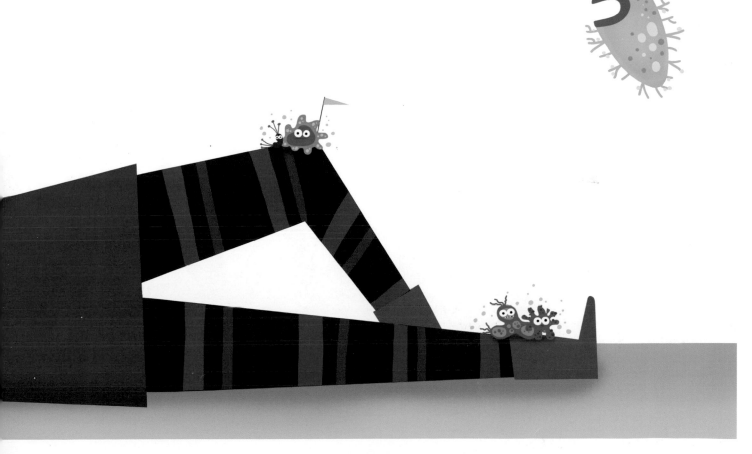

The Skinny on Skin Microbes

When you look at your own skin, it seems smooth — apart from a few bumps and scrapes. But to a microbe, your skin has folds as deep as valleys, cracks like canyons, and dark caves at each hair and pore.

Microbes are everywhere on your skin, but they aren't spread around evenly. Some like dry places, such as the broad, exposed surfaces on your legs and arms. Some flourish in moist areas, such as the crease of the elbow or the space between your toes. And some settle down in oily places, such as the skin of your face and neck. Feet are prime real estate for fungi. One study of just 10 adults found more than 200 types of fungi on their feet! Analyzing their toenail clippings turned up 60 types of fungi, and a search between the toes turned up 40 types. But, surprisingly, the prize location was the heel, with 80 different types of fungi.

You know what they say about mites?

· · ·

Hair today, gone tomorrow.

For skin-loving bacteria, you don't have to look farther than your own belly button. A research team in the United States surveyed the belly buttons of 95 people and found 1400 kinds of bacteria. Most belonged to common species, but a few hundred were unusual and possibly new to science. A few others were downright strange: at least one person was carrying around bacteria that until then had been found only in the ocean.

A couple kinds of mites are particularly fond of faces. They spend most of their lives snuggled down in the warm, moist hair follicles (pits at the root of the hair) on your face. At night, though, when you're sound asleep, a few of them go walkabout. They wriggle out of their homes and wander about on your skin, perhaps in the hope of meeting nice girl or boy mites.

But don't worry. The one thing face mites don't do is poop on your face. Mites hold it all in for their entire lives — which last only about five days. Then they die, drift up to your skin's surface and drop off, poop and all.

Take a Deep Breath

For a long time, most scientists thought there were no microbes in people's lungs unless they were sick. But the scientists were wrong. Lung bugs — well, microbes — are part of a healthy microbiome, too.

In 2009, a researcher in California asked 10 people to cough and spit into a cup so that she could look for lung viruses. She found that all the coughers and spitters had viruses — and plenty of them — an average of 174 species per person. Even more surprising, the coughers and spitters had similar numbers of lung viruses, even though half the people were healthy and half had cystic fibrosis, a disease that affects the lungs.

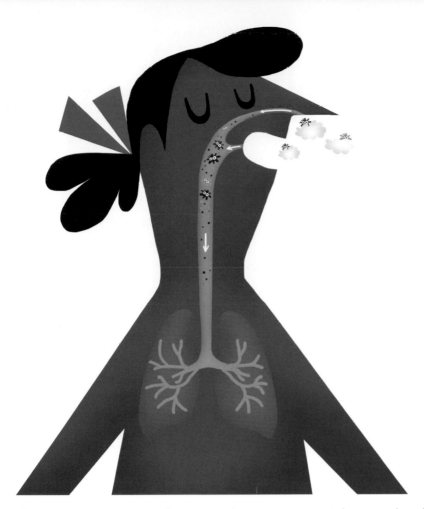

Breathing is a great way for microbes to get inside your body and join your microbiome. Microbes in the air enter when you breathe, but so do microbes from all the surfaces the air passes on the way to your lungs.

Try taking a deep breath. Can you feel the air go through your nose? And you might feel a sort of tickle at the back of your throat as it passes through your mouth cavity to the passages that lead to your lungs. That's how the air going into your lungs picks up microbes from the inside of your nose and from your mouth, two of the most microbe-friendly parts of your body. In fact, many kinds of microbes found in your lungs are the same as the ones that live in your mouth.

However, there aren't nearly as many microbes in your lungs as in your nose and mouth. Your mouth and nose are lined with thick layers of mucus-generating cells that trap dust and protect these areas from drying out, among other useful functions. Many microbes find mucus an ideal place to hang out in, eat, grow and do other microbial things. But your lungs have a much thinner layer of moisturizing stuff, so only tough microbes survive there. In fact, mouth microbes outnumber lung microbes by about a thousand times.

Did You Know?

Colds are no fun, but at least they don't last long. What happens is the cold-causing human rhinovirus attacks the mucus cells lining your nose, causing them to go crazy and produce so much mucus that your nose drips and you sneeze and cough. But you're in luck! Your body normally sheds and replaces those cells fairly quickly, so the cold goes away once the infected cells are gone. That usually takes only a week or so.

In Through the Mouth

Did You Know?

In 1991, hikers in the Alps found the frozen body of a man. Scientists determined that he had died about 5300 years ago — and that he'd had gum disease. They discovered that the poor man had suffered from such a bad case of it that the bacteria had spread all the way to his hip bone.

The biggest collection of microbes in your body lives in your gut. That's the passage that stretches all the way from your mouth to your anus, where poop comes out. And actually, lots of microbes don't get much farther than the beginning of the gut — your mouth.

After all, from a microbe's point of view, your mouth is a great place to live. There's lots of variety in the landscape, from the mucus lining your cheeks, to the folds of your tongue, to the canyons between your teeth. And nutrients they need pass through every time you take a drink or eat some food.

A group of researchers is trying to list all the bacteria that live in human mouths, but it's hard to keep up. Their latest estimate is at least 700 different species, and they keep finding more. But don't worry. Not all of those microbes are in your mouth right now — only 200 to 300 species of microbes live there at any one time.

Plenty of those microbes are good guys. Some protect you from other microbes, and others start the process of digesting your food. But then there are the ones that can cause tooth decay or gum disease. When you brush and use floss to pry out plaque, you're getting rid of a coating of microbes that want nothing more than to burrow into your shiny white teeth and cause cavities.

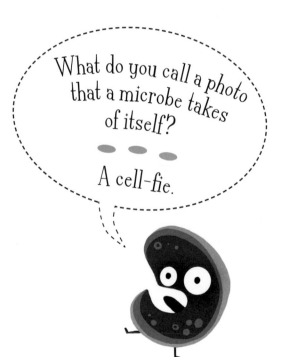

What do you call a photo that a microbe takes of itself?

• • •

A cell-fie.

And you don't always have the same few hundred species of microbes in your mouth — it's a changing population. What you eat can affect it. So can what you breathe in. Even diseases in other parts of your body can affect the microbes in your mouth. Diabetes is known to affect the mix of mouth microbes, but other diseases might, too. Scientists are trying to figure out whether changes in a person's mouth biome might be a way of diagnosing some of those diseases.

And All the Way Through

The lower part of your gut — including your stomach, your intestines and a bunch of other bits — is where your food is broken down into energy and important nutrients. It's also the capital city of your microbiome, with as many as 100 trillion resident microbes!

But they're not just hanging around, freeloading. They're working hard.

Most of the microbes in our guts are bacteria. They break down the food that our own digestive chemicals can't handle and then produce substances that our bodies need. They fight off other microbes that might do us harm. They help us absorb some medicines — and they also help keep our immune systems strong so that we don't need so many medicines.

Gut microbes might even help us cope with some allergies. In a recent study, scientists found that gut bacteria could block peanut allergies in mice. That's a long way from preventing dangerous peanut allergies in people, but the researchers are working on the possibility.

Did You Know?

If your large and small intestines were stretched out straight, they'd be 6.5 meters (21 feet) long — about half as long as a city bus.

Did You Know?

You are what you eat. Or, at least, your gut microbiome is what you eat. You can change the microbe mix in your gut in just a few days by changing your diet. If you eat a lot of meat, one set of microbes will dominate. If you switch to fruit and vegetables, another set takes over. Eating plenty of different fruits and vegetables seems to lead to a nicely varied mix of gut microbes, which is generally considered good for you.

The mix of microbes in your gut is different from anyone else's. It's probably fairly similar to the mix in your family members and the people who live near you, but it's likely quite different from the mix of microbes in someone who lives on the other side of the world or has a very different diet. For example, many people in Japan have gut bacteria that can help them digest raw seaweed, a traditional food there. In parts of Africa where people eat a lot of plants, they have extra plant-digesting bacteria in their guts.

Some of the chemicals your gut microbes produce are used in body parts as distant and unexpected as your brain. In fact, scientists are beginning to suspect that microbes can affect how we feel and how we behave. They have found links between combinations of microbes in the gut microbiome and everything from obesity to depression — and maybe even autism. But it will take a lot more research to figure out how those links might work.

Microbes Fighting Microbes

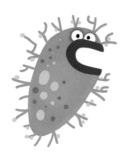

Ever since we figured out that some microbes cause disease, we've been trying to get rid of them. Essentially, we've been tinkering with our microbiomes — although we didn't realize that until very recently, when we began to understand the nature of the human microbiome.

Some of our best weapons against disease-causing microbes have actually been other microbes. For example, a huge breakthrough in fighting disease was the discovery of penicillin. And penicillin was originally produced from fungi.

Single-celled fungi, like the ones that are part of your microbiome, live side by side with bacteria, so they have evolved ways to fight the bacteria off. In 1928, Scottish researcher Sir Alexander Fleming noticed that a fungus was killing off some bacteria he was experimenting with. He figured out how to turn the material the fungus used to do this into a medicine. He called it penicillin.

Penicillin is an antibiotic, one of a group of medicines doctors use to attack bacteria, because bacteria cause many infections and diseases. Since its discovery, more antibiotics have been developed, and they have saved millions of people. But there's a problem. Actually, there are a couple of problems.

First, antibiotics only fight bacteria. They latch onto structures in the bacterium's cell wall and either kill the cell or stop its growth. But antibiotics are like a key that will fit only one kind of lock. They don't work at all against viruses, which also cause a lot of diseases.

The other problem is that bacteria are terrific at evolving. When they are attacked, they can change, fairly quickly, into a form that resists the attack. A lot of bacteria have developed resistance to antibiotics, and the more that antibiotics are used, the better bacteria get at resisting them. If you hear news stories about a "superbug" that is making people ill, that means a bacterium that can't be killed by most antibiotics.

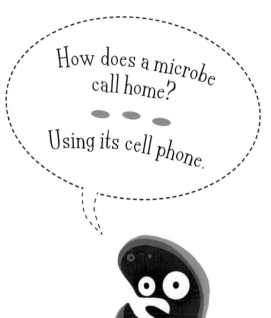

How does a microbe call home?

— — —

Using its cell phone.

Antibiotics may not work against viruses, but vaccination does. Vaccination means giving people a little bit of virus, usually a dead virus, to train their immune systems to fight off the live virus. And it works.

For example, a nasty disease called smallpox used to kill and cripple millions of people around the world every year. Then, just over 200 years ago, an English doctor named Edward Jenner came up with a safe way to vaccinate people against smallpox. More and more people were vaccinated over the years until smallpox simply ran out of victims, and the virus is now considered extinct.

Down the Toilet

Microbe hunters used to have to squint through microscopes, trying to figure out if a tiny, barely visible organism was one they'd seen before or something entirely new to science. Today, microbe hunters have better tools. A lot of them!

Powerful electron microscopes can now actually take pictures of microbes, computers can process huge amounts of information, and — best of all — scientists can read the genetic code of even the tiniest virus.

With all those new tools available, researchers decided to tackle a huge puzzle: the human microbiome. The result was the Human Microbiome Project, launched in 2007. Scientists around the world are working together to identify all the components of the human microbiome and to figure out how they work. The project involves sophisticated technology, the latest computing power, specialized labs — and a lot of poop.

Yes, poop. Science isn't all glamour and clean lab coats. The easiest way to find out what microbes are in someone's gut is to analyze the contents of the person's poop. Poop contains undigested food, shed human cells and lots of the microbes that inhabit your body. In fact, about 30 percent of the solid matter in poop is discarded microbes, and these microbes can be identified through their genetic codes.

Did You Know?

Ever wash your door? It might be a good idea. American scientists analyzed genetic material from about a thousand door frames in the United States. All of them had a thin layer of microbes normally found in animal guts — poop microbes, basically. However, the scientists said there's no reason to panic. Microbes from poop are always floating around in the air. We even breathe them in without getting sick — most of the time.

The researchers started by examining the poop of 200 people, looking for the genetic codes of the microbes they found. Most people, they discovered, have a thousand or so species of microbes in their guts. But not everyone has the same set of species. In fact, every person's gut biome is a little (or a lot) different from everyone else's.

One ambitious scientist is hoping to collect poop from as many as 100 000 people in the United States, and even more around the world. His goal is to get a big enough sample of gut microbes to start building a world map of human microbiomes. So far, several thousand people have actually mailed him little vials of their poop for analysis.

The search for microbes even reaches out into space. Experiments on the International Space Station (ISS) have shown that microbes outside the human body behave differently in space. Without gravity, some change quickly, and some can even evolve into more dangerous forms.

Identical twins Mark and Scott Kelly, both American astronauts, are helping discover how space affects microbes within the human body. Recently, Scott spent a year on the ISS while Mark was living on Earth. Scientists are studying the microbiomes of both brothers — and their poop — to see whether any changes are the result of genetics or space travel.

Save Our Microbes!

So that's you — a whole world walking around, with trillions of inhabitants all dependent on you. And you depend on them, even if you never meet most of them face to, er, cell wall. What can you do about them? Or for them?

For a start, take good care of them. The big thing we've learned over the last few years of research is that most microbes are either harmless or, even better, good for us. And we know that having a wide variety of microbes in and on your body will help keep you healthy.

If you want to attract lots of different microbes to your microbiome — and generally, you do — here are a few steps you can take. Play outside. Explore the natural world. Keep pets. Eat lots of fruits and vegetables. All of these activities will add variety to your microbiome and help it stay balanced and healthy.

Once you've attracted the microbes, treat them well. A diverse microbiome is a happy microbiome.

Clean is good, but not too clean. Avoid antibacterial soaps and shampoos when you can. Soap designed to kill bacteria will likely kill some of your best microbial friends, too. Then the

soap and shampoo get flushed down the drain and kill a lot of innocent bacteria in lakes and rivers.

Don't use antibiotics that you don't need. Let your immune system do the work. The more we use antibiotics, the more chance we give the bad bacteria to evolve a resistance to them. And besides, antibiotics just won't work to cure the flu or the common cold or anything else caused by a virus.

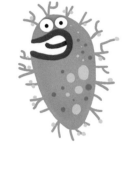

Scientists are looking at ways to encourage the growth of microbes that are good for us. They even hope to find ways to cure diseases by restoring healthy microbiomes in people. But it's complicated. Everyone has a different microbiome, and the difference is big between people who live in very different parts of the world or live different kinds of lives. Besides, not all microbes are friendly. It isn't easy to figure out which ones will live together well and which won't.

Still, researchers are working on some interesting ways to improve your microbiome or fix it if something has gone wrong. How about a cream that nourishes the helpful bacteria on your skin? Or foods that nourish the good bacteria in your gut and encourage new microbes to settle there?

And if your microbiome is damaged and making you sick, you might be able to get a nice new mix of microbes from a healthy person — through a fecal transplant. That means taking some microbe-rich poop from a healthy person and introducing it into the sick person's gut. It sounds disgusting, but it seems to work, at least for some people. Stay tuned!

Glossary

antibiotic: a bacteria-killing substance prescribed as a medicine. It does not work against viruses.

archaea: single-celled organisms only distantly related to bacteria

bacterium (*plural* bacteria): a single-celled organism found almost everywhere on Earth. Bacteria are the most common microbes in humans.

cell: the smallest unit of living things that can survive and reproduce

fungus (*plural* fungi): neither a plant nor an animal but a separate group of organisms. They can be single-celled or multicellular. Yeasts are single-celled fungi, and mushrooms are multicelled fungi.

germ (*see* microbe): any single-celled microbe, such as a bacterium, fungus or virus. Some germs cause disease, but others don't.

microbe (*short for* microorganism): a tiny living thing usually too small to be seen with the unaided eye. It includes bacteria, some fungi, protists and many other organisms, most consisting of a single cell.

microbiome: a collection of microscopic organisms that all live in the same place — on you, for example

phage (*short for* bacteriophage): a virus that infects bacterial cells

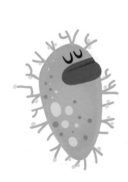

protist: a tiny, free-living organism. It might be single-celled or a bit bigger.

virus: a bit of genetic material surrounded by a protective coating. It is so small, it can only be seen with an electron microscope.

Index

10/16